remember,
please be

komorebi press
London | Toronto | Boston | Tokyo

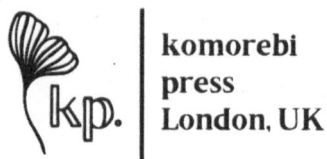

komorebi
press
London, UK

Remember, Please Be
Copyright © 2024 Amy Kirasack
Cover illustration copyright © 2024 Lilly Prinz

All rights reserved

This book or parts thereof may not be reproduced in any form, stored in any retrieval system, or transmitted in any form by any means without prior written permission of the copyright owner and publisher.

Subjects: Non-fiction — Self-help. Spirituality — General.
Spirituality — Non-dualism. Poetry — Contemporary.

ISBN: 9781836022749

Second paperback edition 2025
Printed and bound in the United Kingdom by bookvault

all this —

whoever you are,
wherever you are,
whenever you are,

it's for *You*.

remember, please be

amy kirasack

contents

Epigraph	1
Introduction	5
Part I.	11
Part II.	63
Part III.	113
The Marathon	163
Afterword	171
Meditation on Being	175
Postscript	176

please, remember:

if you're feeling lost
wandering somewhere in the mist
looking for yourself

searching for the Love
that was once within you

your voice
your passion

a memory of brighter days
or spark of spring delight

i just want you to know

i'm here

i'm listening

please, open your eyes

open your arms

it's okay

take me into your heart

and let go.

this is my gift to *You*.

remember, please be

Dearly Beloved,

This book was written for you. It is an expression of my love for you, born from the wellspring of my heart, the same wellspring that runs through all of creation. The same wellspring which runs through you.

Let it serve as a reminder of the essence of who you truly are, which in itself contains everything you've been searching for. For every moment of frustration, of fear, of longing, of feeling something was missing—all of it has lead you here. Wherever you are, whatever you're going through, however you're feeling. Right now. Let it be your anchor through the storm.

You are already whole, already complete. You,

who you truly are, are more beautiful, more powerful, and more loved than you could ever imagine. You have simply fallen asleep to your true nature.

Although the mind may try to lead you astray and convince you otherwise, the very act of continuing to read these words is a reflection of a stirring, a willingness, a desire for repose. It is a fluttering of eyelids, an awakening from slumber within you.

The butterfly is ready to be born.

Turn inwards: rest your attention on this feeling. Remember that this stillness is your essential nature: the stillness from which you arise, dance for a while, then return.

The message conveyed through these pages cannot be found within the words, nor even within their meanings. This is not a text to be intellectually analysed, but an experience to be felt. It cannot be understood by the thinking mind, only held in the heart.

The true essence of what these words imply can

only be found in the spaces between: when you open yourself to inner silence. Even so, this silence, once grasped, is only a pointer—a guidepost on the path towards the light of awareness that illuminates all.

It is a reminder of everything you already are.

This is not a book to read from cover to cover: take the time to pause. Come home to the peace between the spaces. Set it down for a while. Return to these words when you feel called: they will always be here for you.

Whether in nature, on the train, at home, or in a busy café, come back to the breath, and let the inhale lead you to your heart. With the exhale release all thought, judgment, and resistance. Rest awhile and let the silence expand your being. Rest awhile as pristine awareness.

In this moment you will find that this peace is always with you: it is the very fabric of your life, of Love itself. When you are weary, remember to be. This is your essential nature: the very peace from which Love expresses its joy of creation.

Please, feel, within your heart, that you are loved

more than any words could ever express. Know that you are divinely guided with every step on this journey. Remember that whatever storms you suffer on the stage of life, this Love accepts you, sustains you, and cradles you through it all.

This Love is your very nature.

Dearly Beloved,
Remember, please be.

Amy Kirasack
March 2024

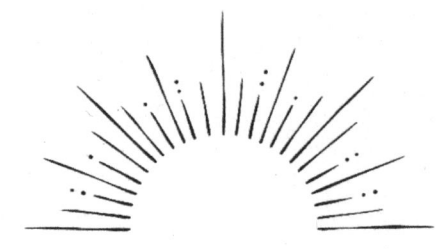

remember
—know thyself—

On knowing.

We move, grow, and are constantly becoming throughout our lives. The circumstances may change: our appearance, our relationships, our titles, our skills, our thoughts, feelings, and beliefs. Arising, then passing away.

It is so natural, so gradual, then, that we never even stop to consider it. Nothing ever stays the same.

Revolving on the stage of life, we find ourselves back where we were before, completely changed. Yet somehow there remains a sense of continuity. A sense that we are connected to the thread of who we were yesterday, who we were ten years ago.

What is the one constant throughout our lives?

What can we truly know, without doubt? What is the light that shines so brightly, that its very being illuminates all of your experience?

This light cannot be found without, in the phenomenological stage of change. Nor can it be found within the mind, which, like its neighbour, constantly dances as a series of ever-changing impressions: thoughts, feelings, ceaselessly flitting memories.

Only deep within. In the repose of silence, in the resting of attention on the very light which reflects onto the world: the very illumination which gives rise to experiencing anything at all.

It is a quality that is so intimate to our being, so intrinsic to life itself. Closer than our very breath.

In stillness illumination arises. In stillness illumination remains.

Ever present, ever aware.

Know: I am.

remember, please be

who am i?

who are you?

are you your titles or your roles?
your ties with those you love
and those you push away?

the bright lights you adorn yourself with
a home, a watch, a treasured heirloom —

are you your eyes or your toes
your thoughts or feelings
the pain and pleasure
of your art and your prose?

could you be the stories
you tell yourself at night?

your past, your troubles
the history of lineage, your genetic destiny
or the hopes and the dreams

of who you want to be?

or are you all of these things —
or none?

one by one
if these shadows should melt away
in the white fire of the sun

tell me, who would you become?

who would you be
naked in the light
of your own Being?

remember, please be

We live our lives entranced by the shadows of the external world. We identify with what we build around us: our relationships with people and things, how we see ourselves, and how we perceive the world sees us. But all of these things are subject to change. Throughout the course of our lives, they constantly evolve.

Before you learned your name, learned to speak and label things, were you still *you*?

Our perception of the external world is coloured by the lens of internal experience: our physical sensations of the body, our emotions, our thoughts. Nothing is constant. The body grows, changes, and is constantly in flux: cells die, and new cells take their place. Our emotions can jump from despair in one moment to elation the next. And a thought can cease, to be replaced by yet another thought.

The very fact you can be aware of these things — that you can observe them as separate — means that fundamentally, they do not define you.

Who are you?

This question cannot be answered with intellect. The mind will respond with thoughts, based on conceptual identifications, which by their nature are ever changing. You are not your thoughts.

What are you?

The moment a thought arises to answer this question, move your attention outside of the thought. Accept that a thought has arisen. Observe it, clearly, for what it truly is. This experience cannot be conceptualised by the mind.

Rest in the observation of both internal and external experience, in clear awareness. If a feeling of annoyance, frustration, or confusion arises, or perhaps even another thought arises, continue to accept them as they come. Gently shift your attention out of identification with whatever arises, and embrace their existence. Stay in the space of your heart. This is your space to be free to respond rather than react.

Feel the space of awareness expand. You are right here.

You've always been the observer.

As with the cycling of the seasons, all of life revolves around the only constant of our entire earthly experience: the light of awareness itself.

amy kirasack

i waited for permission

    to forgive myself for my mistakes
    to set down the suffering i've been carrying

    i waited for assurance

    to be happy with the life i'm living
    to be sure of this path i've chosen

    i waited for someone to tell me

    that it's okay to let go
    that everything's all right
    that i just need to let it flow

    i waited for permission

    until i realised
    i was waiting for me.

remember, please be

When you look outside of yourself for reassurance, you fuel the self-doubt that sustains the ego. The ego, by definition, is an incongruous system: an interconnected network of belief patterns, oftentimes in conflict with itself. It is conditioned into you through experience, forever seeking to add more to itself to bolster its validity. Because it was never real—it was never you.

Seeking affirmation, then, is a reflection of the ego's inherent fragmentation: I am not good enough, people will judge me, I can't trust my own choices. Therefore whatever external affirmation you do receive, it will never be satisfied.

How can you remedy this?

You don't. Trying to *do* something—trying to

quell the ego is like trying to uncover the light of the sun by blowing the clouds away: more clouds will always come.

Just let it be without identifying with it.

Simply rest as the awareness which contains the ego, and see your thoughts for what they are: fragmentary, passing clouds. Let them come, and let them go. Each time you allow them to pass by, you can feel the lightness expand in your heart. The less resistance you embody, the sooner you will realise the clouds were illusory to begin with.

You see, you were never waiting for the light of the sun to guide you.

You were always the sun.

remember, please be

when you feel your old wounds open

    the stinging smarting pain
    the weight of all those staring eyes
    don't turn away again

    remember:

    the caterpillar has to perish
    for the butterfly to be born

The suffering that arises with the reemergence of old wounds means that they never fully had the chance to heal.

Any resistance to whatever arises in awareness: a negative thought, a feeling of unrest, feelings of doubt, judgment, unpleasant situations, anger, a craving for something, can be summed up with the simple words "aversion of what is". Aversion of your current experience. Saying no to the present moment.

When you turn away or try to bury the resistance, you continue to deny what is. The burden grows heavier, and the wounds are etched deeper into the subconscious.

You may not be able to control your external circumstances, or even your thoughts or emotions, but you can choose how to respond to them.

In a way, the very emergence of suffering in awareness is an act of grace. It's a chance to choose differently, to allow the object of suffering to illuminate a path forward.

What is in the way, is the way.

The moment you are aware of the suffering as separate from your true self, the return to awareness itself becomes the space of peace in which to heal.

Now it feels natural to feel gratitude for the opportunity to grow. Tender and fragile, imagine that your old pain is like a small kitten cowering in a corner. How can you welcome the pain, cradle this pain in your heart like a loving mother?

Turn towards your shadows and embrace them in the loving light of awareness. Let them dissolve in your light. In doing so, you shed the old identifications which burden you, and are free to be who you truly are.

Love.

amy kirasack

undergrowth

    whose vines have you covered yourself with?
    whose spiny overgrowth have you claimed
    as your own?
    whose shadows have you hidden behind,
    mistaking them for your scars?

    have you forgotten?

    beyond the clouds:
    there's always the sun

remember, please be

What dark thoughts and toxic beliefs are buried within your subconscious, or swirling around the narrative of the ego mind?

Whether negativity to yourself or to others, the result is the same. Realise that they are not who you are. You do not have to cling to them. You don't have to push them away. You can simply let them be.

See them as they are, dancing on the screen of awareness.

In every moment, you have the chance to realise you are not these shadows. You have the chance to be free. Look back, deeper within: who is the one who observes? Who is the one that gives rise to any experience at all?

The nature of this observer is silent. It's simply

open awareness.

When you immerse yourself in this practice, you begin to see that all destructive action stems from repeated identification with dysfunctional thought: suffering enacting suffering, spread from individual to individual, from generation to generation. You begin to see that we all lose ourselves in suffering in this manner. There is no truly conscious destructive action, only unconscious destructive action.

With every breath, return to the stillness within you. You don't have to choose anger, violence, frustration, shame, or judgment. Know that these impulses are part of your experience, but not *who you are* at your core.

They are are passing clouds, remnants from another identification with separateness. Let them come, and let them go. Let them take their course, as part of nature's play. Until you notice, in a single moment, that they no longer have any form.

Rest. Know that you are home.

remember, please be

tell me:

    how many of your pearls

    are lost beneath a sea of fears

    before they ever have

    the chance to grow

    & how deep will you dive

    to find them?

Maybe you gave up drawing because you were told that you couldn't make a living out of art. Or you stopped swimming because you were the last picked for the team. Or you threw away your dreams of becoming an author because a teacher gave you a terrible grade on a short story.

What joys have you pushed aside, abandoned in fear of judgment, in favour of what was expected of you? What passions have you forgotten about, without ever giving them the chance to bloom?

These gifts are still within you. They're waiting, patiently, deep within, for you to discover them once again. They are pearls of divine light, buried deep under layers of conditioned limiting beliefs.

In order to unearth them, you'll have to venture

into the unknown, and meet the reflections of your false self.

These pearls are gateways to your true essence. Doorways into expression of who you already are. Discover them, and you will reveal the pathway towards purpose.

Because it was never about the praise from others, the recognition you could win, or the money you could make.

It was always about the joy of simply allowing yourself to be—to express yourself in the way that comes naturally. It's what psychologists call flow state, what athletes call the zone, and what artists call the muse.

It's the state of complete and utter being.

Being is your own personal connection to the divine light of peace within you: where thought ceases, time disappears, and you become one with the task at hand.

You become one with now. Before you realise it,

everything just becomes so *effortless*.

It's who you truly *are*.

So dive deep, and follow the light of your joy: it will be your compass through the darkness.

remember, please be

there is nothing

there is no way you need to feel
nothing you need to prove
no titles you need to gain

nothing

no mountains for you to climb
nor battles for you to conquer

there is nothing you need to do
no words you need to say
no one you need to see
nor role you need to play

there is no thing
no one.

there is no one you need to be
only You.

You:

your own flickering light
illuminating
this beautiful tapestry
your life
in its full catastrophe

a beautiful bittersweet kaleidoscope
our lives
this transparent playground of jewels

of all,
of one,
of none.

of You.

remember, please be

A paradox: those who seek it will not find it, but only those who seek will find it.

The more you do, the more you try to find peace through effort, the farther you stray from it. Because the nature of peace is simply being. It is a complete allowance of all that is, being completely in alignment with wherever you are.

How many times have you found yourself listlessly scrolling through your feed or compulsively checking your phone? How often do you "keep yourself busy" to try to drown out the constant chatter of your mind? Endlessly play games or watch shows? Or throw yourself in work or social engagements to ignore a gaping sense of emptiness in your heart?

What are you really searching for? Don't you see? The more you try—the more you disturb the surface of the lake. How can you find stillness, how can you find peace here?

Just be.

Take a deep breath. Drop back inside of you. Deep below the surface is endless stillness. Can you feel it? The more you let go, the more you simply let everything in your stream of awareness *be*.

Trust the process—difficult sensations may arise. You may feel overwhelmed, especially if you have lived most of your life unaware of what lies below the surface. Anchor into presence and recognise the feelings for what are: passing clouds in your awareness. And with every loving embrace of your wounds, they will heal.

Suddenly, you realise: it's you.

You—the very light through which you experience anything at all—were the peace you were searching for all along.

remember, please be

our world can only mirror

    the extent to which
    we allow ourselves to be

    as long as we continue
    to hide behind our masks
    masks are all we'll see

amy kirasack

All of the identifications we have — our likes and dislikes, our roles in society, our personal narrative — when regarded as fact, solidify into the lens through which awareness experiences the world. At this level, we can only interact with others through the ego identity. Through the separation of "me" and "you".

This is not just about the obvious masks: our age, nationality, gender, career, education, or physical appearance. Or even what seems to be more benign: our hobbies, current home, our favourite pair of shoes. Our strongest masks, our most distorting masks, are so close to us, so constant, that for the vast majority of people, they don't realise they are masks: bodily sensations, thoughts, emotions, and the deeply rooted beliefs that underlie them.

When we meet another through these masks, we're always looking at them from the point of view of other. Why do we cling so tightly to our masks, shape our entire experience around our masks, and interact with others only in accordance to our masks? We let the features of our masks become gulfs of difference to push us away from one another.

Why can't they instead be seen as beautiful representations of the diversity, the endless creativity of life? Like the different ways life expresses itself in the millions of creatures in a forest or a sea? Is not our earth and all its inhabitants a macrocosm of the microcosm?

In the space of silence between us, can we sense that everything—all the labels, the illusory identifications, social stratifications, and the space that embraces them—that all are that? Expressions of life— of Love—itself?

As long as we continue to look through these masks, as masks, we are not embodying clear awareness. We are not embodying from the heart.

Realise that the appearance of these masks exists *in* awareness: they are filters, expressions of awareness, through which we interpret all of experience. But they are not *who we intrinsically are.*

How can we meet the world, see it as it truly is, until we see from the light beyond our masks?

remember, please be

all that you seek

    will never be found in the world of forms

    in shadows of truth

    for the entirety of creation

    is the very stillness

    which embraces them

What are you searching for? Is it status? Is it power or money? Could it be companionship? Are you looking for praise or acceptance?

Perhaps you don't know what you're searching for, and you're rapt in frustration. Perhaps you just want to rest. Whether it's consuming or quiet, it remains a whisper in the darkness, a tugging at your sleeve — something is *missing*.

Ask yourself *why* you are seeking.

Don't be satisfied with the mind's first answer, keep asking why. Go deeper. What egoic identification with lack is creating the craving, and how does that reflect the fundamental nature of what you seek?

Peace. Happiness. Freedom. Comfort. Love: safe

in the warm embrace of home. Is this not what you are looking for, at your core?

Have you forgotten?

How many times have you gotten what you wanted, only soon after to find you want something else? That the craving doesn't go away? Because the ego is fed by gain, by adding unto itself more things, more concepts, more knowledge, more experience. As long as you continue to seek outside of you, you only address the shadows of the external world, and not the root cause of suffering: you will continue to feel dissatisfied.

Come back to the stillness within you. Rest awhile as pure awareness, and just observe the pull of craving within you, even if just for a moment. Should you find yourself resisting, then observe the resistance. Feel how the space of your heart expands.

Just be.

Let your actions, unswayed by thoughts, be guided by the clear light of awareness.

The rest will follow.

amy kirasack

the strongest tree

    is not the one
    who defies the storm

    but the one
    who bends with the wind
    and grows taller
    after the squall

Strength is not a refusal of emotion. Strength is not control. Strength is not conquering, subjugating, or destroying our shadows. Doing so is the product of being completely consumed by the ego's resistance: fear, anger.

Egoic aversion sees everything as other: everything as a threat which needs to be defeated. It sees experience—life itself—as something to defy, to defeat.

This is not strength. This is violence. It is a denial of the very nature of life.

True strength rests in complete allowance of what is. Unwaveringly saying yes to whatever difficulties enter the stage of life, and with every squall rising to the challenge with eager flexibility.

Consider: how much trust in life would you need

to completely let go in all of experience? How much courage would you have to have in order to allow, smilingly, everything to come to pass?

Saying yes and accepting does not mean condoning wrongdoing or giving up, or becoming despondent to experience.

It means to fully allow what *is*, while simply being present in open awareness.

How can you let the storm flow through you completely, and not even for a moment flinch? And in doing so, learn to dance with the winds of creation, responding with the flow, instead of struggling against it? By staying anchored, deep down, in the knowing of who you truly are: the light of awareness. Being.

In doing so you allow a greater power of endless compassion to flow through you. You allow this infinite flow to empower you, to guide all your actions through the balance of love and wisdom.

This is the wellspring of true strength, and the very force which gives rise to all life.

remember, please be

we believe for a while

    through the eyes of a single ray of light
    in the shadows on false walls
    rapt in a thousand sorrows and delights

    until the full light of dawn awakes
    and shadows dissipate
    bathing our world in wonder

    blindingly
    we realise
    we were always the sun

When we live our lives through the perspective of the conditioned ego mind, we immediately identify with the labels and judgments placed on experience. Ever changing, ever evolving. Good, bad, pleasant, unpleasant—how could one possibly find peace on an ever-changing rollercoaster of experience?

How can one be free?

As long as we keep continuing to identify with our judgments or emotional reactions, we will be entranced by shadows. It is akin to seeing yourself in a mirror distorted by negative ego patterns and believing that the distorted reflection is reality.

This is not to say that we should completely ignore the conditioned mind. The opposite of losing yourself in ego (complete identification), would be manifested as aversion (complete rejection). In doing so, instead of recognising experience for what it is, the content of awareness, the continued refusal of experience fragments awareness into ceaseless value judgments of worthy and unworthy. It is akin to shattering a mirror and removing fragments that the ego feels aversion to, and believing that the fragmented reflection is reality.

How do we see clearly?

Neither lose yourself in ego nor reject the ego. Observe the compulsive patterns of thought and emotions for what they are, and let them be.

Allow whatever arises. Embrace all experience in loving awareness, and turn your attention back to the peace that resides in the spaces between. In doing so, you realise that you *are* this awareness that pervades all experience, in which ego identity is but an aspect, though not the whole.

Return to being the sun: shining unobstructed, as you always have.

amy kirasack

a process of eternal becoming

    i remember
    i've been here before

    your familiar warmth
    the endless depths of your compassion
    how could i have ever forgotten you?

    my beloved
    who always holds me so dear
    even in the darkest days

    your whispered guidance in my ear—
    open your eyes

remember, please be

The pathless path, as some call the spiritual journey, is never linear. We will remember, we will forget. The road unclear, but the journey endless. We will find ourselves going round in circles, lost in the dance.

But you see, is this not all just part of the play?

Every challenge is a different aspect of the shadows of our subconscious coming to the surface. Do you recognise the patterns in the people, situations, or circumstances in your life? When you regard them symbolically, what lesson could they be trying to bring to your attention?

How can you accept the feelings and thoughts stirred by this challenge, and integrate into your understanding the ways in which your ego mind still entrances you? So that next time, when a similar situation arises, it will slide off you like morning dew on a leaf?

If you reside in every moment within the anchor of stillness, reminding yourself that this light of awareness, so often overlooked, is the one space of peace which can harbour you from any storm, you will know in your heart that you are never truly lost.

With each breath, come back to centre. Leave all the dissatisfaction and constant narration of the ego aside.

In brief moments of lucidity we find ourselves awake. Sometimes this is seemingly the fruits of concerted effort, other times seemingly grace. Continue to open your eyes, and rest in the point of clear awareness.

If you allow yourself to dance without resistance, life becomes play. Joy naturally arises.

This moment extends into an eternal now.

remember, please be

where do i begin?

where is the fulcrum
on which my life revolves

all experience:
the dance of spring delights
or heartbreak of autumn farewells

from where do i witness
these clouds of thought
the heavy scars of
lines drawn in the sand:

not this, not that,
in rejecting, contracting

please this, only that
and in clinging, become them?

let all wash away
in the evening tide

amy kirasack

illusory

under the gaze of the moon

i searched for me within the noise

the chords of falling snow

and found only silence at my core

embraced in endless

light

and now i realise

where do i end?

remember, please be

We divide our experience into internal and external, into "inside of me" and "outside of me". But if we are not the outside world, and we are not our thoughts, emotions, body, or beliefs, where is the inside world?

Where do you start, and where do you end?

Consciousness, that is, the clear light of awareness without thought or abstraction, simply the state of being, arises before any experience can exist. Can you possibly ever experience anything firsthand outside of your consciousness?

You can conceptualise of other experiences outside of your apparent consciousness, but these experiences are secondhand constructs of the past or future. You can postulate of the existence of some form outside of awareness—but the idea itself is an abstraction of the form to which it points, not the form itself.

The experiencer must therefore be here, now, before anything is being experienced at all. There must be the observer before there is the observed. Consciousness must arise before experience. Rest in this notion.

In essence, all that *is* appears on the screen of awareness. It occurs within consciousness. We might be apt to limit the idea of a localised consciousness to what we call "I", but who is "I", really?

This is not an idea to be intellectualised. The ego mind with which one identifies is a limited point of view within awareness itself. It can only be explored through being: through direct experience. Through resting in silent awareness, and, as awareness, exploring what arises.

The wave cannot understand the ocean.

But the ocean is every wave.

can you hear it?

the singing of your heart
is the music of the spheres:

your presence each note
your joy each verse
your love the movement

of this ever-expanding
symphony of light

i'm listening

can't you see, my love?
this universe is yours to create

Let yourself live from that space of joy that is always within you. The love that sustains you, and all life, is ever present.

You need only return to the light of awareness itself: observing, without judgment, all that flows through experience.

The more you surrender, the more you will begin to hear the music. It's faint at first, but then it grows. You realise it's always been here. The primordial vibration of life. It is the very rhythm of your breath, the very pulse of your veins, the very beat of your heart. Feel that warmth grow.

It's you.

There never was any straining, trying, or doing. Those were only identifications with the ego.

Fall into the flow. Let it wash away all your

worries. Wipe away the tears. Bathe in the light of your being: whole, complete. With every expansion let your attention come home to your heart.

From the space of stillness, nature unfolds with natural grace. You see? There's nothing else you need to do.

Just be.

you are the life

that runs through the golden veins of leaves
on branches of the trees
who reach their fingers to the sky

and tickle in the airy stream
the very wind that carries wings
back to their clouded home

how could you be anything else
the very light of Being
you see,
when lost in seas of thought
you lost your summer sheen

there never was a one who *does*

a face behind the masks

the greatest joke — the thoughts were ghosts!

you see?

no one is here

all this only Is

only You, and only Me

who dance in perfect Being

there was no effort to be made

your very nature

green

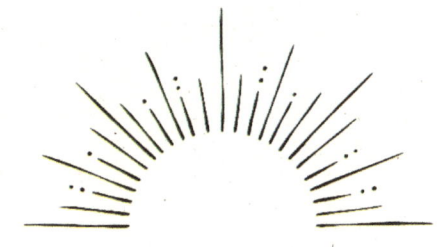

remember

—love thyself—

On loving.

Love is.
We are conditioned to believe that love needs to be earned by the ego: through achievement, through recognition, intellect, beauty, status, wealth, likability—*then* I will be whole. *Then* I will be worthy.

But love, true love, is not a transaction of energy. The transactional nature of what we call love is a mimicry of its real essence. Love is the very infinite source of energy itself.

It simply is. There are no rules, no judgments, no expectations. Only infinite unconditional allowance, like the all-encompassing light of the sun. The loving awareness which creates for every form of its essence a flourishing garden of life. A flower does not need to earn the sun's light, it is by its very nature a beloved creation of life itself.

When you meet others through the mask of the ego, you enact the drama of conditional love. You imply, unconsciously: you must earn my goodwill. You must exchange something of yourself: your time, your wealth, your connections, your contributions—before you are worthy of my love.

Please, come home.

If you simply let go of these masks—if you let the light of your awareness shine through the ego identifications of separation, letting all aversion and clinging dissolve—you fall back into your true nature. You embody from the space of loving awareness.

And you wake up and finally see: that Love is always right here. Always within you.

Because the truth is, it's never really about the things you do. Or even the words you say. When all is said and done, people will remember you for the way you made them feel.

Can you extend to others freely, the light of Love

that underlies all life, that illuminates all experience, to their very core?

You see, you don't need to *do*. You don't need to strain to shine this light on others. The more you try, the more you cling to your masks and identify with needing to be something other than you already are. The more you try to impress or play intellectual games, the more you cover your light in false shadows.

You don't need to try, because you *are* it.

Come back to centre: to the breath, to the body. To let your attention reside in your heart, and let go. Realise that you are, in your essential nature, already an expression of this Love. Just let it flow through you.

Be the space of loving awareness.

The way a flower can spread a smile in the heart of a passerby, your loving presence will lighten the hearts of everyone you meet. You only need to bloom into what is already inherent within you.

Beloved, please be.

amy kirasack

dearly beloved

wherever you are
i'm here —

with every breath
i'll welcome you
so close your weary eyes
and come home

however you are
i'm listening —

with each beat of your heart
feel the nectar of my embrace
humming
a sparrow's lullaby
as i trickle down to your toes

whenever you are
i'm now —

remember, please be

don't worry, child

i'll cradle you in dappled sunlight
weave wind through tears and laughter

as you dance among the garden
of your own creation.

Over time, the wandering wears us down. The constant pressure of our lives, the uncertainty—did I take the right turn? Should I have gone left?

Venturing into the unknown, the untrodden path—to where your heart has been calling you all along, but the mind kept telling you no. No, it's unreasonable. No one will care. No, you can't go on this way.

The amount of courage and vulnerability it takes to follow your heart in the face of all odds—it's crippling. It hurts because you have to let go of the old you: all the things that never served you, all the limitations that held you back. Transformation is painful. It takes time.

But you're not alone. You're never alone. The

remember, please be

Love that has guided you here continues to sustain you—please, just listen. You knew how to before: in childhood, in simpler days, when everything was just play.

Fall back into the stillness of your heart. Rest a while, and know that *I am*.

Let the flow, in every moment, carry you to where you need to be. Know that whatever meets you on the journey, no matter how terrifying or painful the process, is all part of your growth.

Take a deep breath down to your core. Feel the life flow through your veins. Stay right here, in the open space of the heart. Let the mind talk. Let your body ache. Let your emotions swirl. Welcome all in the loving embrace of awareness.

Slowly release your breath and let your heart expand. Be this moment, right now, and let the wind carry your wings above the horizon, through the clouds, dancing in the sky. You're free.

You see, none of this was ever meant to be punishment. It's your chance to learn. To grow. To delight in your own creation.

amy kirasack

when the roaring strikes you

and raging winds surround you
don't lose yourself in the fear

come back to centre
breathe into me
your anchor through it all

i'll take your hand
and lead you to
the calm within the storm

remember, please be

Every moment of doubt, every moment of fear, is another chance for you to discover the compass within to guide your way.

Whatever happens, you can always return to your awareness. Awareness itself is a clean slate: the clear light of experience. Its nature is acceptance. It illuminates, without discrimination, whatever comes its way.

So fall back into this awareness: observe, without clinging or aversion, the internal and external world. You don't have to do anything. Just let it flow through you.

Rest in this moment.

Remember, you have always been this very anchor within you. Any emotions or thoughts will cloud your ability to see what's in front of you, but bringing your attention to rest in the space of the heart, grounding yourself in the breath, will guide you through the chaos. The one space of complete calm, like the eye of a storm.

Because it was never about the destination, or some imaginary idea of the future. You only ever experience now. The ability to find peace in any situation rests on the clarity of presence you embody right *now*.

Where are you, right now? Can you bring yourself, in this moment, back to the present?

So trust each step you take, even if you don't know where you're heading. Let every action come forth effortlessly from this clarity of awareness, unswayed by thoughts or emotions.

This is your compass: complete presence.

Soon, you will find that you're already here.

remember, please be

sepia-toned horizons

    over sandcastles and make-believe
    days tinted with dreamsicle cream
    playing in a world of wonder
    with only you by my side

    where have you gone?

    have i grown too old for games?
    or, somewhere along the
    Duties and Obligations
    and Very Important Responsibilities

    did i just stop listening?

The very joy of play you felt as a child was a nudge from the divine. But as we grow up, as the memories of wonder begin to fade, we start to believe we're too old for games. Our world has no choice but to mirror our beliefs. As soon as we give up play, all we see is work.

But you see, the joy of life is never about doing what you ought to, should, or are expected to do. These are words the ego uses to keep you stuck where you are.

If you feel resistance to where you are right now, take a deep breath. Come back to centre and fall into the space of your heart.

Ask yourself, gently, why you continue to listen to the thought patterns which brought you here in the first place? Doing so will only perpetuate the same experience.

True freedom can't be found in the external world. You have find it inside of you first, and let go of the old narrative.

You can decide right now, to change your story.

When you give yourself permission to come back to the endless sense of wonder you had as a child — the infinite play, the joy of discovery, complete absorption in now — your perception of the world will start to change. Things are lighter, easier.

When you give yourself permission to embrace the child still within you, you heal them of their scars. You give this child the opportunity to be heard. To express, to explore, to completely immerse themselves in experience.

To play.

Come back to effortless flow. Welcome home.

amy kirasack

fear

    inside every roaring lion

    is a kitten whose paw

    has been pricked by a thorn

What is fear, but the egoic belief in separation? The visceral contraction at the thought of an unknown other. Not I, and therefore a threat. Other than me, and therefore capable of hurting me.

When you witness an act of great rage, know that this comes from a place of great fear. Traumatic scars in the subconscious that caused the individual to believe, at their core, that the world is a hostile place. That they must bite back to protect themselves. In this manner, deep rooted fear can build a shell of anger around itself for protection.

When you notice a resistance in your emotional process—and this can be as subtle as a quiet hum of hurt, guilt, judgment, fear, or annoyance—let your attention step out of it. Rest in the space between, rest as pure awareness. Simply allow it to be without pushing it away or becoming identified with the process. Be aware of the experience and watch as it unfolds.

See it for what it is: a conditioned emotional response. Any time you feel yourself being pulled away, come back to the feeling of pure presence. Just observe. Allow the resistance to take its course: sensations may rise, grow stronger, and start to overcome you. The more you observe the sensations, the more they will lose their sway over you.

Simply stay as the anchor of awareness, bringing your attention to the breath leading to your heart. You are at peace in the open space of the heart.

Could you imagine how someone else, who, unconscious of their emotions, might have become swept away by their sensations, and reacted with retaliation? Are we not all the same?

How can you feel the love of another—or even your own love—if you're afraid to open your heart?

remember, please be

i see you as you are

    in your beautiful catastrophe

    wild, unrestrained & free

    for you to rest in who you've always been

    brings you home to be

amy kirasack

When we look at a tree, we don't think: oh, this tree is wrong. This tree is bad. It should be taller, straighter, or healthier.

When we look at a tree, we see it as it is, why it is: from the environment around it, from the way the rain fell, from the way the sun shone. It grew according to its nature, not due to effort or straining or judgment of self and others.

We allow the tree to be.

Why, then, do we look at others and identify with the ego's judgments or expectations of them? Is it, perhaps, because we cling to these judgments and expectations of ourselves?

Can we simply allow ourselves and everyone we meet—to just be? Have we not all grown according to our nature, to circumstance, doing the best we could?

Can you see, that when all trees are allowed the space to grow according to their nature, they create a forest so lush in variation, so teeming with endless new discoveries, and so rich in different points of view?

The next time you find yourself clinging to a thought or belief, step back and see it as it is. Momentary, passing impressions. Notice the space between awareness and the object of awareness, and let it be. When you give yourself the space to simply be, you embrace all of you.

You are truly free.

Know, Beloved, that whatever arises, internal or external, nothing can ever extinguish the light of the sun.

In residing in this loving awareness, you will find, that over time, your very presence becomes the nourishing space for others to grow freely, too.

To rest at home in being.

amy kirasack

the love you're searching for

can't be found outside
in reflections

only inwards:
rest in your natural state
of wholeness

what wants not
needs not
resists not
and is not

your perfect stillness
where love begins to dance

remember, please be

Self-love might make you think of sea salt baths and massages or an afternoon spent napping on the beach.

But is that all there is to self-love? Or is that just rejuvenating your body? These activities alone may help relax you, but if your mind is constantly racing, and your thoughts polluted with anxiety, the mind will return to this maladaptive state soon after the the body falls back into its old patterns.

Who are you, really? If you are not your body, your emotions, or your thoughts—then how do you love yourself? Where are you?

What is the one act of self-love that you can return to at any moment, regardless of your external circumstance? The one act that will bring peace not only to you, but extend to those around you?

Come back home.

By returning to the point through which all experience occurs—the point of awareness, and simply resting there in your heart, without resistance, you will soon experience that the very nature of this awareness is loving. It is peaceful, it is complete.

In allowing your attention to rest as awareness, free from clinging and aversion, you allow yourself to embody the sun, bathing in the light of love which nurtures you.

This light of alertness, of being awake—the sense of actually *being here* right now will allow you to truly be present in the world. Aware. Listening. Feeling.

Being.

Watch as the world becomes brighter, more colourful, more beautiful in your presence. How could you have ever overlooked it before?

The peace of your being will radiate into the hearts of others, allowing them, whether consciously or unconsciously, to be touched by the same infinite warmth of compassion.

remember, please be

i picked up the shards

of the broken words
we threw at each other
the tears we shed
and put them back together

and all that reflected back to me
was love

When we hurt one another, it is not from a malice intrinsic to the individual. Those who instil the most suffering have often suffered greatly themselves, knowingly or otherwise, and have acted from a place of complete identification with negative egoic patterns.

Can you think back to a time when you hurt another, and are ashamed of yourself now because you know better and no longer identify with the past version of you who behaved in such a manner? Do you see that at that time, you were completely identified with the thoughts, emotions, and beliefs of that stage of your life?

Let go of the burden of guilt: you acted only according to your limitations. You needed to make mistakes to grow.

Now, can you bring that same forgiveness—that same loving presence of allowance—to people who have hurt you in the past?

You don't need to condone their actions. You don't need to agree with what they did. But can you extend that same space of compassion for others to change, as well, and in doing so, liberate them?

In doing so, liberate yourself?

Often the most unconscious actions of others, the ones that give rise to the greatest suffering, can become our greatest opportunities for growth. They challenge the boundaries of the ego identity and create the deepest wounds, which, once given the space to heal, become our greatest strengths.

Beloved, can you hold all the pain and suffering of your life—the times you hurt others, the times others have hurt you—within the light of awareness in your heart? Can you see that we are all just doing the best we can, bound by our limitations?

Can you see now, that you are free?

I'm sorry, please forgive me.

Thank you.

I love you.

Feel the burden lift from your shoulders. Feel the lightness swell in your heart.

Observing all life, ever-present, is the warm embrace of unconditional Love.

remember, please be

tidal

when the wave comes
embrace the crest rising in your heart
let Her hum submerge your toes
reclaim your essence whole

each exhilarating crescendo throws
your soul into the flow
of thrashing water sprays
a glittered sunset's rays
over light refracted droplets
suspended on the horizon
to crash beneath Her endless depths
and release you floating to the troughs:
a drifting breath's repose

just close your eyes
and trust Her arms
to bring you back to shore

The trials and tribulations of life will come in waves, in cycles. If at first you don't integrate the lesson—if you try to swim around it, push it away, or if you try too hard to defy it, conquer it—it'll come back again. This time in a different form. Taller, wider, rumbling up from the ocean floor.

You can't escape the wave. You can't defeat the wave. The only way is out is through: to release the tension in your body, respond to the rising waters, and be fully present right now. The more you let go, the more you can listen to its movement. The more you can embody the flow.

This isn't an idea to be conceptualised: it's one thing to read these words, nod at a few interesting notions in them and then return to thrashing about in

remember, please be

the sea. You see, it's a practice to be lived. It can only be felt through direct experience.

It can only be embodied in the now.

Let the challenges of life flow through you, embracing the highest highs and lowest lows, all the while continuing to be anchored in the sense of presence. Don't lose yourself in the crashing waters. Stay here. Stay in the breath which animates you, in the expansion of your heart. Let yourself be immersed in the full catastrophe of experience.

Let it guide you.

At the top of the crest, the fresh sea salt air filling your lungs, it's clear: this isn't punishing. It's exhilarating.

Fall into endless expansion.

With every wave, allow the seas to cradle you back to shore.

amy kirasack

at first, you locked me in your heart

a choking pain, too many tears
nestled warm within your darkness
shut away inside your fears

the tides in turn
carry my cries back to you:
an echo you shoulder
the ache in your chest

can't you see?
you've just gotta let me grow

embrace each wound inside
let every scar illuminate
with each layer brilliance rises

until i bloom in your embrace
dancing among the waves

a single laughing pearl

remember, please be

Our deepest wounds shut away inside our heart, once tended to, become the catalyst to nurture our greatest strengths.

Whether you were the victim or the perpetrator, let down the burden of guilt. Of regret, of anger. The more you resist and construct walls around experience, the more you build a tangled web of egoic blame, multiplying your suffering.

Why are you reliving your pain, listening to your ego tell the old story again and again? The more you push against something — the more you shut it out — the more it will accumulate, underneath the surface, until it bursts in a relentless surge, overwhelming you.

Hold the object of your pain in awareness: realise it is there, that it is worthy of your attention.

Although it is not you, it is not other than you. It is part of you.

Realise you did your best at the time: you reacted in the way you did according to your level of understanding at that point of your life. You did what you did because you didn't realise that you *are* the very space of awareness which can choose to respond, and not react.

The nature of life is Love. Ever forgiving, ever compassionate. You have the chance, each moment, to choose differently. To choose to embrace all in compassion.

This moment is a gift: the present. It's an opportunity to let go. To heal.

Honour this moment. Greet your scars with warmth and understanding. Allow them to dissipate in the presence of your awareness. Welcome them home, to be.

In doing so, you grow the pearls of wisdom from your suffering, layer by layer. One you can share with others to guide them on their journey, too.

remember, please be

please cry, my child

    let the tears become the flow
    to let your grasping sorrows go

    and bathe your weary heart in light
    reborn in wide-eyed wonder

If we allow ourselves to process our emotions fully, it does not mean we will feel no pain. Pain is inevitable, but suffering, optional.

When you feel yourself being overcome by a wave of difficult emotions, come back to centre. Bring your attention back to the space in the middle of your chest, and from that space, without thought, judgement, clinging, or aversion, become aware of your emotional process. Feel everything in your body. The pain, the physical strain, the choking in your throat, the rattling of your heart, the shaking of your breath.

Let it flow through you.

Throughout it all, be the anchor of your awareness. Who you truly are. Realise that these sensations are storm clouds passing by the sky of

remember, please be

experience, and you are the light of the sun.

Allow nature to enact its purging process through you. In letting the storm pass freely, you continue to be present as the bright awareness of the sun throughout any and all experience.

No amount of rain, wind, or clouds can ever touch who you are at your core. Be still. Know that Love is holding your hand, every step of the way.

In every moment you let go of what burdens you, you allow the storm to take its course and the clouds to dissipate. In turn you allow your essential nature to arise: to be reborn clearer, lighter, and brighter than before.

amy kirasack

the beauty of this bittersweet

a fervent longing for your Being
so far—my Own embrace

just stay awhile
in fragile nectar
and drink its warming gaze

for when I give Myself to You
the separation fades
and so We find Us face to face

and laugh—ironic!
wouldn't you say?

for when as One
without the distance
the bitter can't remain
so holding Me whole in Your arms

is only Bliss in plain.

remember, please be

The ups and downs of our lives give us the very range of emotion that colours human experience. How beautiful it is to be able to taste the nuance of the bitter juxtaposed with sweet!

Without sorrow, we would not know joy. Without fear, we would not know love. From the point of view of the mind, we only recognise the light because we have experienced darkness. We only know duality.

So when you grope in the darkness alone and searching, know that the very appearance of darkness requires the awareness of its opposite: light.

Set your eyes on the inner light of unity: on wholeness. This is your very nature, a wholeness that can only be felt.

You will find, that when you meet your essential

nature: the Love who looks though your very eyes, closer than your breath, that it is with you at all times. In the space between thoughts, in the silence between words. Forever guiding you, patiently, giving you the space to grow.

You see, this Love is always with you, for it is the very essence of your being.

Rest in Love, and only Love remains.

remember, please be

when you learn to listen

it's like jazz, you see

you can only begin
to embody the flow

when you let yourself
fall into the river

Silence is the language of Love.

When you listen, you reside in the space of inner silence within your heart. This is your natural state of being. Listening—true listening—does not speak, does not judge, does not try to change the other, and does not try to do anything.

It simply *is*, remaining still as the surface of a lake on a sunny day, so that all that impresses upon it can be reflected in their clearest state.

True listening allows all that comes to pass to be reflected without resistance. When you resist, you create ripples, or even waves, and thrash about on the surface of awareness.

How can you perceive clearly the person who is in front of you, or the experience in which you are immersed, if the surface is not still?

With the return to silence within you, you are able to embody the flow of life more authentically as a force that flows through you, as you, in its full expression.

You are no longer a dancer performing on a stage, you become dance. You are no longer a musician playing music, you become music. With each repeated surrender, you create in harmony with this divine intelligence: half-written, half-improvised.

In this allowance, there is an unconditional acceptance of what is. This is the nature of Love. It is a complete and permeating *yes* to all of experience. An allowance of nature to unfold. Unwavering in its glow.

Be the flow of life in its full catastrophe, in its endless beauty.

amy kirasack

love is not a currency

it's a state of being

love is not a currency
not a practice nor exchange
love is not the fruit of deeds
nor appraisal to be gained

love is not conditional
nor cowers in the night
love is ever present through
your eyes, its very light

in perfect stillness
love can grow
& bloom in glowing bliss
inherent in the seed

you see,
love was never found without
for it's your very being

remember, please be

The sun does not discriminate when it shines its light. There is no such thing as those deserving and undeserving of its warmth: such a concept is born from the egoic belief in separation.

Separation implies competition, hierarchy, winners and losers. It implies rules for love, conditions to be met. Worthy and unworthy. Some for you, none for you, and a little more for you. This is the current accepted paradigm of love on which the ego operates.

Tell me, how would you want to be loved? Do you want to endlessly struggle to prove yourself worthy of love? Are all not one dance of creation under the light of the sun?

The sun shares its light, as this is its very nature.

It does not diminish in brightness when it shines upon another. It does not need to practice shining its light. It does not need to make any effort to be. It simply is.

This is the very light of awareness that animates you. The very essence of everything within consciousness, of Love itself.

When we identify with the masks of societal expectation, cling to fear or judgment, or become consumed in egoic thought patterns, we forget that we are this light. When we continue to seek the fulfilment of our heart in forms outside of ourselves, we are continuing to perpetuate the feeling of lack inside. That we are not worthy. Incomplete. Unlovable.

The truth is, you don't need to *do* anything to be. The very fact that you are here, now, experiencing reading these words, this book in your hands, is proof that this light of endless compassion animates all of your life.

Whether the thinking mind believes this statement or not, turn within, and from this stillness ask your heart: do I want to be enough?

You already *are*.

Give yourself permission. Simply remember who you've always been: that space of stillness inside of you. Let the chatter of thought, the chaos of the world be. Come home, right now, to this very moment.

Be as you are: Love.

it's like jazz

like love poetry
the songbird's melody
or a sleeping kitten's purr

can't you see?
it's all part of the process
each time a little better
each time a little bit more

you've just got to let it *flow*

with the soft summer breeze
or chamomile tea
like the scent of sweet roses

you've just got to let it *grow*
because it's really that simple

the sun's fingers through your hair

warm sand between your toes

can't you see?

i just wanted to remind you

of that three letter word

— — —

it's you

this is how much

i just wanted to remind you

of those three little words

it's always you

just these three little words

this is how much

i love you

please be

—be thyself—

On being.

You already know how to be.

It's about settling back into your true nature, into what you've been all along. About waking up from the dream of separation: of being entranced by your thoughts, feelings, and beliefs.

It's so simple, yet somehow so difficult, for the mind to truly grasp—because the mind, by its very function, is the antithesis to being. If the ego mind absorbs all of one's attention, the very underlying foundation of *I am* disappears. The observer becomes the thoughts, becomes the chaotic emotions, becomes the dysfunctional patterns.

Even so, grasping this concept intellectually is akin to studying music theory for decades without ever having touched the keys of a piano. The mind has to fall away, to relinquish control of attention, in order for your being to fully shine through as the light of awareness.

Step out of your mind, if just for a moment. Ground yourself in the sensations of the breath, in the space in the centre of your chest. See if you can notice an expansion in your heart as you drop into your breathing. Simply allow attention to rest there, and from the heart, look out into the world.

No past, no future. No thoughts, no judgments. Allowing everything as it comes. Simply being. Can you feel the rhythm of life as it flows through your heart?

Can you observe the inner world unfold around you, in perfect succession, without getting swept away in its dramas? Can you see beyond your masks, your egoic beliefs, to meet the outer world as it is, and always has been?

Can you behold whatever is in your experience right now, in the light of endless peace, to simply allow everything that comes to pass, to be?

Can you allow the light to grow, to engulf you fully, to expand so wide, that it opens within you the endless wellspring of peace, embracing everything in calm stillness — that you can't tell where you begin, or where you end?

This is who you are. This is the true nature of being.

You may feel a cool tingling in your heart. An unravelling of tension, a release of emotion. It may create shockwaves under the surface, rattling you to your core.

Let it be. Let it wash over you, for you are the very anchor through the storm.

There are trials yet to face, and mountains yet to climb. But you are facing the most important moment of your journey now, as you always have been.

This very step, right now.

Beloved, come back to be.

amy kirasack

whenever you're ready

there's a seed of truth within you
that only wants to grow
that begs the warmth of your attention

whenever you're ready
to spread your branches
for the flow of your intention
to reach beyond who you were yesterday
to blossom forth as whole

whenever you're ready
and your heart is ripe with endless wonder
your buds bear fruit
radiating with your irreplaceable sweetness

to bless all who have been waiting for you
above all

Your own Self
all along

remember, please be

Whatever resistance you feel, however slight, is a gentle reminder. Like the ringing of a bell, nudging you back to centre.

When you resist, you push away what *is*. You're either lost in thought about the past or the future. Lost in the story of the small you, the one the ego keeps clinging to.

You've forgotten who you truly are.

Come back to right now. Come back to be.

The more you rest in being, the more you nurture the seed of truth within you: it is your own unique expression, your own beautiful mode of creation. The profound gift that comes naturally to you, that brings you into the state of flow. This is your gift to the world. Will you let it grow?

The very fact you are here, now, means that you have a purpose. There is meaning to your life. In so many countless ways you may never understand. That your very existence, your very presence, is so crucial to the endless lives reflected in your being.

The world is waiting for you.

Every moment, every breath you take, is another chance to nurture this presence of awareness in you. To come back to the sense of wholeness in your heart, unswayed by the outside world. You don't need to do anything other than be.

In resting as this awareness, your gifts—your purpose will start to flow through you effortlessly. Take each step from the space of this awareness, ever listening, ever awake.

Whenever you're ready, you will naturally bring the fruits of your gifts to bless the world.

remember, please be

with every twirl i surrender myself

to your song
delighting in our play

how can high can i climb?
how far can i run?
how wholly can i lose my way

so when i find my way back to you
our joys multiply again?

There is a common misconception that every time you forget yourself in meditation, every time you lose yourself in thought, you've somehow failed. That it's a sign you're not suited to it. When in actuality, that's the entire practice — of not only meditation, but of life itself.

For without these moments, how would we learn? Does the sculptor not have to chisel away at the stone?

Every time you lose your way and become controlled by thoughts in awareness, entranced by the shadows of the mind, you create for yourself another opportunity to grow. The moment you find yourself again — the moment you realise where you are, gently bring yourself back to centre. Back to the light of awareness that you are. Let yourself sink into awareness. Rest in stillness, simply observing the thoughts and feelings. Without identifying or pushing them away.

From this space of stillness, immerse yourself fully into experience. When you feel the burden of life weighing you down, when your legs become weary, you can always come back to the divine light of awareness that is ever with you.

From the deepest depths of despair, or the highest peaks of exhaustion, breathe into the space of your heart. It's always here for you. Let peace surround you.

Let the light fill your entire being.

With each repeated reunion, you will be more intimately anchored to the Love inside you. So that each time, it will become easier to find your way home.

amy kirasack

torrential

she's shouting at the rain when i find her
spring showers not enough
to cope with her tears
as i call to her —

*why yell at the rain
when you can just carry an umbrella?*

but when she turns, she only laughs —

*why carry an umbrella
and miss the chance to swim?*

remember, please be

The point of view of the stories we tell ourselves shape our experience. From the point of view of the ego: oh, it's raining, what a terrible day. From the point of view of flowers: oh, it's raining, what a wonderful day!

When you allow everything to simply be, without clinging to a point of view, experience softens. This, in fact, is clear seeing. You begin to observe the world—the events, the places, and people you meet—from the light of acceptance. You rest in a space where you can chose to see difficult conversations as a chance to learn, or an inconvenience as an exciting detour.

Come back to the stillness within you to hold experience in compassion. Within this stillness, you can begin to become aware of the limitations that distort your interpretation of experience.

What story would you rather choose?

One that contracts you, debilitates you, and makes you the victim? One that requires shielding yourself from experience or fighting back?

Or the one that expands you, empowers you, and excites you? One that allows you to play, gives you space to grow, and unite all together as one?

Ultimately, you are free to choose. This is the boundless loving nature of life itself. Whatever you choose, you will be divinely supported.

You see, you are already free.

You always have been.

Can you feel the gratitude flowing within your heart? With every moment you can choose anew the light with which you meet the world.

This light becomes the very music of your of life.

remember, please be

our earthly kingdom falls

when our great cities of concrete
constructed towering over
lampposts of artificial light

and grand bridges of steel
with our oil devouring machines
begin to show their cracks

who will greet us once again
but the smallest green-leafed friend
awakening to the laughter of the sun?

wherever you stand
is all not embraced
under Her warmth?

There are no worthy or unworthy creations under the light of the sun.

In some forms you may be able to see the light of Love with ease: the natural state of inner peace grows freely from their very being. The light is so clear to see in nature, in animals, in small children. A sense of clarity of being, of the thread of the divine.

But you see, even the seemingly cold machinations of human creation are also a reflection of this divine Love. They are an expression of the infinite variation of creation itself. However disconnected from nature they may seem, can you not give all equally the unconditional awareness of the sun?

Can you extend this not only to the objects, but to the experiences in your life, to the people you

remember, please be

meet? However you may feel about them from the egoic point of view of separation—however distasteful they may seem, can you fall back into the space of loving presence within you, and see them as they are? Beautiful expressions of life?

Simply let them be?

However you may feel about yourself—the harsh words the ego throws at you, the shame or guilt or feelings of inadequacy— know that you are part of this infinite creation.

Can you simply let yourself be?

We build our kingdoms, then let them fall. Throughout the rhythm of history the light of life itself will reclaim them all. Returning, with Love, our creations to the earth.

To rest, to be reborn. To create anew.

amy kirasack

in your eyes

    i see the very light
    i hold within my heart

    in your voice
    i hear the chimes
    of the bells calling me home

    and in your arms
    i float on the cool winds
    of endless compassion

    the very essence of life

remember, please be

When you live in every moment from an authentic state of loving awareness, an interesting shift may begin to happen. The same loving awareness from which you observe the world will be reflected in the world back to you.

The greatest gift you could give to another is not material. Things change, memories fade, but only love remains. The greatest gift you can give another is the loving attention of clear awareness: truly seeing them, as they are. The light which underlies all life.

When you serve another, you serve Love itself.

If you find yourself in the presence of another, whether a loved one, a friend, a stranger, or even someone you're not particularly fond of, hold their being in your awareness. Embrace their presence warmly. Look into their eyes, and see them as they are: not as their outward appearance, not as the egoic character which they play, but the life which animates them.

At first, this may seem uncomfortable, unnatural. But know that it is the ego that regards the other as threatening, as something to be feared, that urges you to turn away.

Simply reside in the open space of your heart, unswayed by thoughts or judgments that may cloud the mind. Hold the individual in your awareness. See if you can meet the light behind their eyes that is ever present in a state of complete peace.

This is the recognition of Love: the wholeness which underlies all creation.

What you recognise in another, you can only do so because you have experienced it in yourself.

remember, please be

how much more can i let go?

    with each surrender
    i give to you
    the seeds of worldly deeds

    i cast each breath
    throw overboard
    each burden to the sea

    let truth's sweet syrup
    glowing bright
    your sunrise, golden gleam:

    to let your presents
    flow through me
    and trust your growing green

    on waving branches
    cradled tight
    your lullaby, the stream

Being is a process of letting go. Of opening yourself up to all experience, of learning to trust in whatever comes your way. The greater your trust, the more fear and resistance fades.

You let go because you realise you don't need to cling to things. They always change. You don't need to push things away. They always change. It was never the things themselves that brought you peace: but the internal feelings of peace they inspired within.

The peace that was already within you. The peace that is always right here.

When you have the chance, go out into nature. Observe, from the space inside your heart, how all of nature rests in a perfect state of being. There is a stillness in the spaces between that is anything but empty. Instead it teems with a divine intelligence. The trees don't worry. The flowers don't judge. There is no doing, no trying. They simply let themselves be: and all growth, all beauty, emerges effortlessly from that being. Let nature be your guide.

Stay present, allowing your own self, and everything reflected within that light, to be.

With each breath you entrust a little more of your false self—the worries and the tears, the judgments and the fears—to the flow of life. Surrender them, simply watch them float away. They will come, and they will go. As the seasons, let them swirl around you.

Because the very light of your being, of Love itself, has always been your solace. Always been the foundation of life. When you simply let yourself drift into the flow, the stream of awareness flows more freely: more gently, with more lucidity.

Let the light illuminate your path forward. With every breath, know that you are cradled by the stream of creation.

listen

it's not about
the words we say

but the space we hold
between them

remember, please be

The quality of presence that you are able to embody in your interactions with others expands the space not only within your own heart, but within the hearts of those around you as well.

True connection is not made from the thinking mind. The ego subsists on separation and will always regard others as separate from it. When you regard someone as "other", they are automatically evaluated in comparison with you.

How can this person hurt me? How can this person help me? How will this person judge me? How can I impress this person? How can I make this person feel better? How can I benefit from this person?

Interaction is no longer about the clear illumination of the person in your awareness, and instead reduces the interaction into a means to an end in relation to the egoic lens of self.

When you are able to sit with another without thought, judgment, or preconceptions, simply residing as the pure light of awareness, you allow them to reveal their true nature. When you open your own heart to receive, authentic vulnerability allows awareness to regard the content of awareness—the other person—as no longer other than you, but of you.

In doing so you hold them within the loving awareness that you truly are. You meet them in the light of presence you share with all life. In listening to another, you open your heart to accept them wholly and unconditionally, as they are.

You give them the space and the warmth to express freely: to bloom.

To be.

remember, please be

each moment

    is another chance to forgive
    to let go of the chains that bind your heart
    or the fears that shroud your shoulders
    the nightmares that cloud your eyes

    this moment
    is another chance to release
    to surrender the stories you tell yourself
    of sorrows, unhappy endings lost
    the words you left unsaid

    because right now
    is my gift to set you free:
    a single spacious breath
    to bathe your heart in stillness —

    this single silent breath
    to lead you back to me
    to where you've always been
    all along.

In moments of stillness, can you sense the eternal patience of Love? How infinitely forgiving, how ever gently Love guides you on your journey?

When you realise you are lost, you have already escaped the shadows of despair. You have awoken from the dream, and can start to see confusion for what it is: the ego's identification with suffering. You are free to come back to awareness in a single breath.

If resistance arises, you are given another moment. And another. Always, only now.

Do you feel the relentless surge of the stories you tell yourself, the judgments, the painful thoughts crowding your mind? Is it anger? Fear? Aversion? Perhaps shame or guilt?

Please, step out from the chaos. Every moment,

you can choose to be free. See that you can stand at the water's edge and simply observe the thoughts as they ebb and flow.

With the inhale into your heart, feel the presence of Love embracing your sorrows. Accept them, welcome them, as of you, as guests in your space of awareness—but not intrinsically *who* you are. And with each exhale, let go of what no longer serves you. Let them rest a while, and, when they are ready, let them be on their way.

Wake up, Beloved.

Wake up to the infinite light of awareness, the very Love that animates you. The Love that has never left you, and has held your hand through it all.

amy kirasack

eight billion mirrored pearls

winking countless
waves of crystal dewdrops
laughing in the sky

each light echoed by a neighbour
returned tenfold in smiles

each one suspended in your own heart
on a canopy of shared dreams

who usher you to sleep
with a glittered lullaby

scattered whispered over eyelids:
goodnight, my love
goodnight

remember, please be

However you're feeling right now, please know: you're not alone.

Your life is not in isolation. The very fact you exist means that your life is reflected onto the life of another, and another, which in turn reflects the lives of countless others, forming an infinite network of the life which animates the world. The light of awareness which allows us to experience anything at all.

That you are here, right now, means that your being, no matter how seemingly insignificant, is an integral note that sustains the symphony of creation.

Remember.

When you reside as the loving presence that you truly are, open to whatever comes your way, you expand the light around you. You free others of the constraints of their masks. You become the space for others to reveal their true nature and express freely.

Can you feel it?

There is an openness, an ease that emanates from your loving presence, and others will innately sense this light. The clarity of your awareness ignites their own, allowing you to meet in the space beyond thought, beyond judgment, and beyond separation.

In the space of pure being, all can meet as we truly are in the light of Love.

As one.

With each smile you share, you light another candle to illuminate the darkness. With every loving thought you embrace, you embrace the entire universe.

remember, please be

i speak to you in many ways

    it's ceaseless:
    every day

    through the sunset's tickled rays
    or a stranger's knowing smile
    a laughing friend or waving fern

    in time with seasons' winking turn

    a whispered frosted leaf
    the sound of footsteps giving way
    to winter's silent sleet

    i'm here
    around you, everywhere
    i'm in your very breath

    if you could pause and stay awhile
    in time
    between your words

The guideposts along the way are so obvious, so plain to see, that you can easily overlook them. Consumed by endless thoughts and emotions, the fog of the ego is so thick that often you can't see what's right in front of you.

We are all one. Choose love. Be yourself. It sounds so simple, but it's true. The best hiding place has always been in plain sight. Your real purpose, the real reason you're here—is to just *be*.

You're already being.

You suffer in being when you identify with doing: with pushing things away or clinging onto things. Consumed by thoughts churning through your mind. Regretting the past. Waiting for external circumstances to change. Delaying your happiness.

Wherever you are, whatever you're going

remember, please be

through—give yourself the chance—the *space*—to breathe. Come back, just for a moment, and let the thoughts, the feelings, the discomfort, the pain wash over you. Let them flow through you, the anchor through it all. Let them trickle back to the sea. Let them go.

Let yourself be.

Your being—your true being, the light shining through the life in your eyes—is ever present. It's ever with you. It is reflected in everything you experience, which glows with the same light of loving presence.

In a sense, it's all there is.

If you're feeling abandoned, lost, and waiting for a sign, please know that Love has always been whispering to you. You never—not even for a moment—have to walk this path alone.

Listening can only happen in the now. Simply turn your attention away from the chattering of the mind and let the silence—let Love—guide you.

amy kirasack

in every sigh

    i become the rhythm
    of this eternal dance

    with each contraction
    i run to you
    steeped in salted tears
    let it be the sea's
    gentle kiss
    to wash away my fears

    until i jump into the depths
    and lose myself in play
    expand the endless
    oceans wide
    grow greater every day

    the back
    then forth
    sweet calming breath
    each moment

remember, please be

ringing clear:

this rhythm becomes the song
to melt into
your rocking arms
and for while

we're one

your loving echoed
beating heart
sustains my very own

Can you begin to embody your light of awareness in every moment? With every breath you take, wherever you are, whatever you're doing, can you come back to the awareness of who you truly are?

Allow that awareness to contain everything in your experience. To cradle all in the love of simply being. Let that anchor of awareness behold whatever activity you embody in the present moment.

Put away your screens, your books, turn off the music. Whatever action you take: whether walking, waiting in a queue, sitting on the bus, or even something as mundane as housework—give it your full attention.

Simply be.

Suddenly, activities that used to bore you

become opportunities of great expansion: how deeply can you immerse yourself in the task at hand? How much can you let go, to simply be the awareness, accepting everything as it comes, neither clinging nor rejecting whatever comes your way, internal nor external?

You will find that as you reside in this sense of simply being at all times, the world may take on a vibrant glow. Richer, more beautiful. Somehow more harmonious. Everything suddenly seems more alive.

But you see, this is your natural state of being. The more clearly you let the light of awareness illuminate through you—the more you can *be* who you are—the more clearly the world can reflect in you, and meet you in the very light of Love.

amy kirasack

it's not about trying

it's about doing what comes naturally

beloved,
can't you see?
i just want you to be

free

from what ifs and should haves
from afterthoughts and holding back

the more you think
and more you try
the more you leave your Self behind

for who are you,
but Being?

come back to me
safe in your heart

remember, please be

and look — with open eyes!

there's so much waiting here
for you to share
in your own precious way

your seven-layered prism bright
to paint a cloudy day

S ometimes it's the smallest things we do in life that can make the greatest difference. It's never about the grand gestures or elaborate plans. It's about the seemingly inconsequential moments, the things that come so naturally to you that you don't even notice—that can have the greatest impact.

The compliment you gave someone going through a rough time that brightened up their week. The meal you brought for an ill friend that gave them comfort. The vulnerability you shared with a stranger when you wrote about your struggles with depression online, that helped them turn their life around.

There is an endless multitude of ways that our actions create ripples which spread out to touch the hearts of millions. No act of kindness goes unnoticed.

The beauty is that the magnitude of your impact doesn't have to correlate to the effort. It's just about learning to trust what comes easily to you. Your own unique mode of expression, your own way of being that is so everyday, so mundane to you that you don't even recognise them as gifts.

It's that sense of ease, the sense of lightness that comes so naturally to you that the mind goes quiet and time seems to slip away. The very act of immersing yourself in awareness automatically brings you into being.

It doesn't matter if it's dancing, cooking, making people laugh, or even something as simple as listening to others—give yourself permission to fall back into your joy. Let that joy continue to radiate from you and carry into every moment, with every breath.

Let it illuminate the hearts of everyone you meet.

When you live from the space of being, you embody the flow of life itself.

amy kirasack

little bud

little bud,
who are you searching for
leaning away from the sun?

don't you know
you have to bloom
before the bees will come?

remember, please be

When we look outside ourselves to fill the emptiness we feel in our hearts, we decorate the ego mind with more and more, strengthening its hold over our true nature. More status, more money, more things, more friends, more pleasure, more comfort, more adoration, or more experiences. We constantly crave, and we constantly seek.

And yet, even once fulfilled, something feels wrong. Something is missing. We blame others, we blame ourselves. Still, we are not satisfied. So we continue searching.

Ever changing, and ever fleeting, these worldly shadows enter and exit the stage of life, and the ego latches onto the newest promise of eternal happiness: if only I achieve this title, then I can rest. If only this person loves me back, then I'll be worthy. If only I could have solitude, then I'll be at peace.

What you've been looking for was never found outside of you. It was never the external goal you sought, but the feeling you convinced yourself the goal would bring you. You see: you were mistaking the entrancing glow of the *goal in awareness* for the very *source* of the light which illuminates it.

Where can you find the feeling you are searching for?

Only in the now. Come back home to this source of awareness. This is the light of the sun within you. You're already that: you're already whole.

Can you clearly behold, in loving attention, whatever is happening right now? Without clinging or pushing away? And in doing so, be completely present in this moment?

Can you be here, right now?

When you wholly devote yourself to whatever task is at hand, you begin to realise you can access this peace regardless of external circumstances. You become effortlessly present: the flow of life itself.

You see, your purpose in life is not about *what* you're doing, but the state of presence from which you *are*.

Beloved, just be.

Once nurtured, residing in this sense of peace will become effortless. This effortlessness will allow you to grow in a way unique to you. Grow, and express yourself as you truly are, in a voice that only you can embody. With the nectar that only you can create.

The fruits of the flower inherent in the seed.

In full bloom, the bees will come: to delight in your warmth and share your honey with the world.

how do i embody love

in every moment of my life?

be as the sun:
shine your light
loving presence

be as the river:
let it flow
allow everything

be as the sparrow's melody:
let your song unfold
express freely

be as the seed

who grows into the tree

infinity

the truth is

you already know how to be

it's who you *are*

remember —

please *be*.

remember, please be

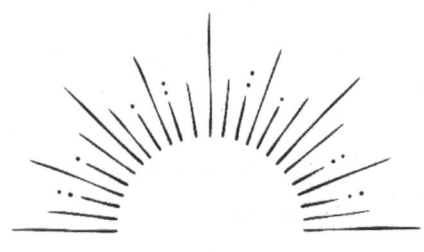

the marathon
—for Dave Evans—

whose light touched so many

and whose courage inspired me to find my voice again

5th October 1963 — 2nd December 2023

the marathon

for Dave Evans

in, out

left, and then right

your eyes on the sun above the horizon
the crisp, cool morning air embracing each breath

in, out

left, and then right

you know where you're heading
you've been here before:
and you'll come round again
the love that you are will never leave us

in, out

left, and then right

like a flame flickering in the wind,
once shared, grows steady
each wick a heart touched by your kindness
each candle another life, warmed in your presence

in, out
left, and then right

it's funny, you see,
because you don't need these legs to run
listen —
can you hear them?

the cheers of those you've guided in your life
thanking you for your love and encouragement
becomes the breath within you
ignites the light within you

in, out

some say courage is overcoming fear
or pushing it aside without giving it a name
but you know
you know
courage is this:
it's here, now
with every breath, every sweet surrender

in, out

each breath a gift:
the present
each moment a blessing
each shared smile a miracle
each laugh a treasured friend

in, out

so don't look back
run on, bright light

because it really is that simple
it really is

in, out

run on, bright light
breathe softly, bright light
you're already home.

remember, please be.

remember, please be

Dearly Beloved,

There is a light that shines within your heart. It is the very essence of what animates you: the breath within your lungs, the warmth of your hands. The entire universe behind your eyes.

It is beyond measure, beyond description. Beyond language. Beyond anything the human mind could possibly comprehend.

It is the beautiful, infinite force of creation that you share with all life.

Know that whatever dark paths you might find yourself stumbling through on your journey, you are never lost. This light is always within you.

For it *is* you.

Whenever you feel the pull of suffering tug at

your heart, whenever you find yourself longing for a home you can't remember, just come back to these pages.

Please, stay awhile. Take a deep breath, and let the love behind these words nourish your soul.

Remember who you truly *are*.

Know that you're already home. That your very nature is to grow. You just have to let go. To learn. To laugh. To thrive as you are.

I just wanted to say thank you.

I am so grateful for your presence. For the ways in which you simply being here has touched hundreds and thousands and millions of lives in ways you may never understand.

Thank you for your curiosity, for your vulnerability, and for your courage every step of the way. Thank you for your loving attention, for your openness to receive, and for your unwavering faith in everything this journey will bring. Thank you for your unique point of view of this universe that only you can express.

I am eternally honoured to serve you in this

chapter of your life.

Thank you.

Thank you for being you.

Please, wherever you are, remember that this Love is always inside you. Remember that these words are simply the pointer to your greatest guide: the light of compassion which is your very essence. Who you always have been, and who you truly are.

Let your light shine upon the world.

May your heart always be open, and may your mind always be pure. May you guide others on their way home.

Dearly Beloved,

May you always be.

Amy Kirasack

March 2024

remember, please be

my beloved,
Please, let me fall more freely into the flow of your endless compassion, and in my surrender, wash over me, bathe in light the false shadows which entranced me, the suffering in my search for you, having forgotten who I truly am. For in every breath I come home to the space within my heart, to let you fill me with the clear light of your Being, so that I may overflow with your Love to greet all in this moment with the lucid, calm clarity of your presence. And through your Being, may I rest as one with your stream that sustains all life, and cradled in your arms allow all to express freely the very same wellspring of gentle awareness: the loving, infinite illumination of the sun.
beloved, i am.

amy kirasack

about the author

Amy was born in Canada to Southeast Asian refugees and spent much of her life country-hopping between America, Singapore, Japan, and Spain, and her more recent years career-hopping from English teaching to software engineering. After her struggles with chronic depression spurred a long and winding journey back inwards to where she began, she finally became ready to listen to her joy and started creating to help others.

She is the host of the *Remember, Please Be* podcast and co-founder and director of Elowyn Community, a charity dedicated to making wellness and holistic practices accessible to all. Between her travels, she is currently based in London, England, where she spends her time co-creating music and holding community events.

@amykirasack
@elowyncommunity

www.amykirasack.com
www.rememberpleasebe.com
www.elowyn.community

amy kirasack

remember, please be audiobook

Narrated by the author.

Get your copy of the audiobook at:

rememberpleasebe.com/rpb-audiobook

remember, please be

ready to shine together?

Scan the QR code above or visit

elowyn.community/events

to join us for our upcoming events.